Families: Using Type to Enhance Mutual Understanding

by Charles W. Ginn, Ph.D.

CAPT

CENTER FOR APPLICATIONS OF PSYCHOLOGICAL TYPE, INC.
GAINESVILLE, FLORIDA

Published by
Center for Applications of Psychological Type, Inc.
2815 N.W. 13th Street, Suite 401
Gainesville, FL 32609-2815
(904) 375-0160

Edited by Thomas C. Thompson, Ph.D.

The publisher gratefully acknowledges the assistance of Production Ink, Gainesville, Florida, for the design, production, and printing of this title.

Printed in the United States of America.

ISBN 0-935652-26-4

Acknowledgements

I would like to thank my wife Janet, and our sons Patrick and Brendan, for giving me the opportunity to experience the many wonders and joys that flow from being part of a loving family. Thanks are also due both of our extended families for the love, support and the many happy moments we have shared together. Of the many titles we may seek in life, I consider none more precious than "Dad."

I would like to express my appreciation to Peg Black, Bonnie Mack, and Dan Roche of the Archdiocese of Cincinnati Family Life Office for their contributions to the development of this book and the *CAPT Family Relations Program*. Dan and I first shared the vision while Peg and Bonnie helped make that vision a reality.

Many thanks go to Tom Thompson, Jamelyn Delong, Glenn Granade, Mary McCaulley, and Jerry Macdaid whose many contributions are reflected throughout this book and the *CAPT Family Relations Program*. Their unswerving support sustained us through the numerous Program revisions.

Most importantly, on behalf of all those who contributed to this book and the *CAPT Family Relations Program*, I would like to thank in advance the many engaged couples and family members who will use these materials as they strive to better understand and accept themselves and their family members. We trust that our efforts applying the MBTI and type dynamics to enhance mutual understanding among family members would be well received by Carl Jung and Isabel Myers.

Archdiocese of Cincinnati Family Life Office

The **Archdiocese of Cincinnati Family Life Office** is responsible for developing and conducting marriage preparation and family enrichment seminars and programs. The staff of the Family Life Office played a vital role in the development of *Families: Using Type to Enhance Mutual Understanding* and the companion *CAPT Family Relations Program.*

CAPT Family Relations Program

The ***CAPT Family Relations Program*** includes 16 seven page individual type descriptions and 136 seven page paired descriptions. Covering all possible combinations of MBTI personality types, the paired descriptions address the impact of type dynamics on effective communications between any two individuals. The individual and paired type descriptions are provided by CAPT in the form of a set of reproducible masters.

Contents

Introduction vii
The Myers-Briggs Type Indicator 1
Personality Type Theory 3
Personality Preferences 3
The Four Scales of the MBTI 4
Extraversion/Introversion 4
Sensing/Intuition 6
Thinking/Feeling 8
Judging/Perceiving 10
Personality Types 12
Most and Least Preferred Functions 12
Cognitive Orientations 13
Quick Reference Guide 14
Listening Across Type Differences 17
Communicating Across Type Differences 19
Reminders for Communicating Across Type Differences 20
Family Norms 23
Understanding the Sixteen Types 25
ISTJ 25
ISFJ 26
INFJ 27
INTJ 28
ISTP 30
ISFP 31
INFP 32
INTP 34
ESTP 35
ESFP 36
ENFP 38
ENTP 39
ESTJ 40
ESFJ 42
ENFJ 43
ENTJ 44
Conclusion 47
Appendix 49
Further Resources 51
Background Notes 52
Most and Least Preferred Functions: Quick Reference Guide 55

Introduction

The importance of families as a cornerstone of society has received renewed attention during recent years as a result of changing demographic and social trends. Our concept of the term "family" has expanded to include families with stepparents, those with adult children, single parent households and many other configurations of related individuals.

Functioning effectively within a family unit requires the ability to communicate with a number of diverse and unique individuals. This manual is designed to help you better understand and appreciate the variety of personality preferences held by members of your immediate and extended families. Often, some behaviors associated with personality preferences are experienced only after you have been in a family for a period of time. Understanding and appreciating the diverse ways people interact with each other may reduce the number of family disputes caused by a lack of effective communication and mutual understanding.

Personality preferences, as identified by Myers-Briggs Type Indicator (MBTI), can help explain diverse behavior patterns. The MBTI identifies sixteen different personality types, or ways by which individuals prefer to interact with others.

As you explore the diversity of personality preferences and how they help identify an individual's preferred ways of interacting with others, keep in mind that there are no right or wrong preferences. No one personality type is better or worse than any other personality type.

One way to better understand the concept of personality preferences is consider how we favor one hand over another when we write. Even though people who are injured in an accident can learn to write with their less favored hand, they normally return to their preferred hand as soon as circumstances permit. In a similar fashion, even though we function regularly in all of the personality preferences to be explored in this book, we tend to favor certain preferences over others. Just as we want to be able to live and work in our preferred functions, it is equally important to give our loved ones the space and permission they need to follow their own personality preferences. We can attempt to influence spouses or children to mimic our preferences, but sooner or later they will want to be themselves.

Be bold and accept the gifts of personality type that God has given you and empower your loved ones to celebrate the gifts of personality type God has given them.

The Myers-Briggs Type Indicator

The Myers-Briggs Type Indicator (MBTI) is a questionnaire that was developed by the mother and daughter team of Katharine Briggs and Isabel Briggs Myers. The instrument is based on the personality type theories of Swiss psychiatrist Carl Jung. Katharine and Isabel created the MBTI so that individuals could recognize and appreciate their preferred ways for interacting with others.

A key aspect of the MBTI is its non-judgmental nature. The MBTI was grounded in the belief that while different approaches to interacting exist among individuals, no one given set of preferences is better or worse than any alternative set of preferences. Thus, the MBTI does not attempt to change behavior to meet a given ideal, but rather encourages individuals to understand and appreciate their own and others' personality preferences.

Since its introduction, the MBTI has become the most widely accepted psychological instrument in the world for use with the general population. For example, in 1992, the MBTI was completed by over 3,000,000 people in numerous English-speaking countries. French, Spanish and other versions of the MBTI have recently been developed. The demonstrated usefulness of the MBTI to help people understand behavior ensures its vitality for years to come.

Personality Type Theory

Personality Preferences

The MBTI focuses on various personality preferences. A personality preference may be thought of as a certain manner an individual finds comfortable when processing information and/or interacting with others. It is important to keep in mind that a personality preference is indeed nothing more than a preference. Personality preferences do not dictate nor in any way control our behavior. Indeed, any number of factors may influence someone to function in a given instance in a manner inconsistent with a personality preference. Family members often strive to create an atmosphere of acceptance in which loved ones feel comfortable functioning within their personality preferences.

One such preference explored by the MBTI involves a person's preference for focusing on existing facts and concrete realities or for focusing on future possibilities. For example, two sports fans who happen to enjoy concentrating on existing realities might enjoy a heated discussion of the statistical performances of certain baseball players. In contrast, several other fans, who prefer to focus on possibilities, might choose to discuss the future potential of the team's rookie players. However, nothing in Jung's type theory or the MBTI suggests that the performance-oriented fans cannot enjoy discussing a player's potential or that their possibility-oriented friends are unable to analyze a player's batting slump. Both groups can enjoy existing facts and future potentials; each group simply prefers to focus on one option at the expense of the alternative.

Another way to think about personality preferences is to compare them to habits. Perhaps you enjoy having toast and orange juice for breakfast most mornings. However, on occasion you like to prepare bacon, eggs, and grits. Clearly, your habit of having toast does not prevent you from preparing a full breakfast. If you really wanted to, you could prepare a full breakfast every morning. In a similar fashion personality preferences indicate what we would like to do, not necessarily what we will do on given occasions.

4
FAMILIES: USING TYPE TO ENHANCE MUTUAL UNDERSTANDING

The Four Scales of the MBTI

The MBTI is composed of four dichotomous (either/or) scales that address certain personality preferences. These scales are as follows:

Extraversion — Introversion
Sensing — Intuition
Thinking — Feeling
Judging — Perceiving

Extraversion/Introversion

The extraversion (E) and introversion (I) dichotomy focuses on our source of revitalizing energy. An analogy to a battery may be useful to understanding the concept of revitalizing energy. When a battery is attached to a charger, energy is flowing into the battery. When the battery is powering a light bulb, energy is flowing out of the battery.

The extraversion-introversion MBTI scale helps identify the settings in which energy is flowing into or out of our internal batteries. Energy flows into extraverted types when they are around people. Energy flows out of extraverted types when they are quietly reflecting on issues. In sharp contrast, energy flows into introverted types when they are able to reflect quietly, while energy flows out of them when they are interacting with others.

The extraverted types' desire for continual interaction can extend beyond the physical presence of others. For example, extraverted types tend to run their televisions even though they have no intention of watching them. The televisions simply provide stimulation.

Introverted types get a "charge" in situations that permit them to organize their thoughts without constant interruptions from others. To better understand this need for a quiet place, it is important to differentiate between loneliness and solitude.

Loneliness involves an absence of others when we would choose otherwise. Loneliness is a condition that all of us, regardless of our personality preferences, tend to find discomforting. Solitude, however, involves a physical setting that enables people to reflect on their thoughts. A place of solitude is a positive place, not a place of sadness. Extraverted types, with their powerful need to be in the presence of others, tend to have a difficult time understanding how some of their relatives might enjoy places of solitude.

As mentioned above, introverted types tend to seek out quiet places that permit an inflow of revitalizing energy. They desire an atmosphere in which they can think through issues and organize their thoughts. Unlike their extraverted type relatives, introverted types can be very content in quiet houses with all the appliances turned off except for the lighting necessary to read and reflect.

Since they depend on a variety of others for revitalizing energy, extraverted types tend to want to spend as much time as possible with as many relatives as possible. Introverted types may also enjoy the company of extended family members, but tend to want more time alone with just their spouse or children.

It is important not to confuse extraversion and introversion with the concept of sociability. Extraversion and introversion focus on where we become energized, not on our degree of social graciousness. Extraverted types and introverted types may be equally refined (or equally deficient) in their interpersonal skills.

Extraverted types are prone to evaluate their self-worth through the eyes of family members. As a result they often seek positive reinforcement from relatives. Indeed, it is not uncommon for an extraverted type to ask, "Unless you tell me, how am I supposed to know that I am a valued person?" Extraverted types sometimes express concerns that their introverted in-laws don't care about their accomplishments if the in-laws don't express such sentiments verbally. It is helpful for extraverted types to understand that introverted type in-laws are not withholding support or recognition; they simply do not share, or understand, the extraverted types' desires for expressions of verbal encouragement and praise.

Introverted types tend to assess their self-worth from a more personal perspective. As a result they have less need to receive verbal reminders that they are valued. Introverted types enjoy being told they are loved, but prefer that such expressions be given in more private circumstances rather than in the presence of extended family members.

Extraverted types frequently share the most intimate details of their personal lives with extended family members, friends and even causal acquaintances. Introverted types are much more selective about those with whom they will share their personal matters. Introverted types are often taken back by the degree of disclosure demonstrated by extraverted types.

Once they become comfortable with new family members, introverted types will join in family discussions and more actively participate in family events. Extraverted types need to give their more introverted relatives adequate time to adjust to family norms and traditions.

In the United States extraverts outnumber introverts by a three-to-one margin. Introverted behaviors such as being reflective are therefore often labeled by extraverted types as being shy or quiet. Extraverted types need to recognize and appreciate the introverted qualities of being thoughtful and reserved just as introverted types need to recognize and appreciate the extraverted qualities of gregariousness and of reviewing issues with others before making decisions.

Sensing/Intuition

Sensing (S) and intuition (N) are known as the perceptual functions since they focus on where we concentrate our attention. Jung indicated that individuals choose between focusing on existing facts and realities (sensing) or on future possibilities (intuition). Since we used the letter I to signify introversion, we use the letter N to signify intuition.

Sensing types find it relatively easy to handle enormous amounts of detail and are often able to recall facts and figures with amazing accuracy. Intuitive types are often surprised when sensing family members are able to spot misspelled words after only several seconds.

While comfortable with facts and details, sensing types tend to dismiss anything that cannot be processed in the here and now. If something isn't real, sensing types seldom consider it important. Thus, sensing types often have little interest in, or tolerance for, hypothetical possibilities that are not grounded in existing realities.

Those who favor intuition prefer to focus their attention on numerous possibilities. Intuitive types like to consider what the future may be like, rather than concentrate on existing realities. While sensing types often concentrate on the five bodily senses, intuitive types tend to focus on aspects just beyond physical reality. Because of this "sixth sense" aspect of intuition, intuitive types are often comfortable following hunches without relying on facts to guide their actions.

Many sensing types subscribe to the conviction that if things are not correct (completely accurate), then they are clearly incorrect and need to be made right. In contrast intuitive types have much less concern with absolute accuracy.

To intuitive types it is not so much a matter being correct or incorrect as it is a matter of being "close enough" or "too far off." Intuitive types tend to leave it to others to define their own parameters for "close enough." This intuitive perspective on the necessary degree of accuracy often causes negative reactions by sensing types, reactions that intuitives may have difficulty understanding.

To better understand the different focuses of sensing types and intuitive types, consider what might transpire if several individuals were walking in a park on a beautiful spring morning. The sensing types would probably bask in the beauty all around them, including the freshness of the breeze against their skin, the beauty of blooming flowers, and the gentle singing of nesting birds. Meanwhile the intuitive types could well be planning upcoming summer vacations. Later, during their summer vacations, the sensing types would probably focus again on the beauty surrounding them, while the intuitive types might already be contemplating their winter holidays. For many intuitive types, once possibilities become realities they lose all interest. Often sensing types will ask their intuitive oriented partners, "Can't you just focus on today for once?" The intuitive types might look back in wonderment and ask, "Why?"

Intuitive types frequently feel frustrated when family members won't join them in contemplating what "might be" in the future. They may accuse their loved ones of being "too concrete" or "stuck in the present." In a similar fashion, sensing types may consider intuitives out of touch with reality. Sensing types frequently question how the intuitives' many future scenarios can possibly become realities. Sensing types may have a difficult time remembering that intuitives don't expect all of their many visions to materialize. Intuitives are not as concerned with whether the future possibilities turn out exactly as anticipated. To intuitives, their visions involve what *could* happen, not what necessarily *will* happen. To sensing types these visions are what intuitives say *will* happen. Communications often break down between intuitive types and sensing types on this *could vs. will* dimension.

In the United States sensing types outnumber intuitive types by a three-to-one margin. Sensing types need to appreciate the contribution intuitives can provide in clarifying what might develop in the future, while intuitive types need to appreciate the ability of sensing types to add substance to visions.

Thinking/Feeling

The thinking (T) and feeling (F) personality preferences focus on how we like to make decisions.

Those who favor the thinking function prefer to base their decisions on objective criteria. They want to address issues in a logical, rational, consistent manner. In order to achieve desired results, thinking types progress systematically through each aspect of issues and then come to conclusions based on what meets, or fails to meet, the criteria. For example, thinking types will approach family problems by determining the relevant factors, identifying alternative courses of action, analyzing the alternatives, and then suggesting which options the family should consider. During this process they will strive to remain objective.

We should not underestimate the importance of objectivity and consistency to thinking types. For example, if you asked your mother-in-law who favors the thinking preference to do a special favor for your spouse, she will probably give a great deal of thought to how her other children might perceive her granting your request. She will want to please you, but won't want to be seen as giving special favors not extended to other family members. Thinking-oriented parents often go to great lengths to spend the same amount of money on each child or grandchild for birthdays and other holidays.

Those who prefer a more subjective approach to decision making favor the feeling function. Feeling types tend to place greater emphasis on the impact of decisions than they do on the objectivity or consistency of those decisions. For example, even though feeling-oriented parents strive to treat their children in an equatable manner, they are much more likely than thinking-oriented parents to make exceptions for what they consider to be special needs. Parents who favor the feeling preference are prone to make exceptions to a child's bedtime or other family rules. "Oh just this once" is an often-repeated phrase among feeling types, while "a rule is a rule" is a more common assertion among thinking types.

Whereas thinking types work through issues in systematic, logical ways that are easy for others to understand, feeling types tend to skip from one idea to another in ways that are hard for others to follow. Thinking types often become confused when feeling types jump from issue to issue without any bridge between the two topics. A thinking type may feel compelled to ask a feeling type, "How did we all of a sudden jump from a discussion about skiing in Colorado to a review of the merits of Idaho versus Iowa potatoes?" Feeling types make such transitions in their heads all the time; they just forget to bring their discussion partners along with them.

Although discussions with thinking types are normally easy to follow, thinking types are usually not as sensitive as feeling types to the impact certain words or phrases may have on relatives. Feeling types are more likely to recognize the subjective impact certain words might have, while thinking types may simply not understand why they are misunderstood so often. For example, a feeling type might be sensitive to the need to treat a new 35-year-old son-in-law as an equal, whereas a thinking type might logically assume that the new son-in-law should be addressed in the same manner as the rest of the boys in the family are treated. Such well-intended consistency can lead to difficulties in an extended family.

Feeling types often perceive thinking types as being insensitive, whereas thinking types tend to view feeling types as hopelessly subjective. Spock and Dr. McCoy from the popular *Star Trek* series personify this difference in approaches. Spock, with his emphasis on being logical and objective, prefers thinking, while Dr. McCoy, with his focus on the subjective ramifications of decisions, prefers feeling. Since Spock and McCoy seem to represent the extreme ends of the thinking-feeling dichotomy, it is not surprising that many people find the character opposite their own preference to be very objectionable.

It is important not to confuse the feeling function with emotions. Both thinking types and feeling types experience similar emotional reactions to major events. For example, thinking types and feeling types may be equally devastated by the death of a family member, but may express their emotional reactions in very different manners.

In the United States the ratio of thinking types to feeling types is about even. There is some evidence to suggest women are more prone to favor the feeling function while men tend to favor the thinking function.

Thinking types need to appreciate the ability of feeling types to anticipate the impact decisions might have on others, while feeling types need to learn from thinking types to remain steady in the face of conflict.

Judging/Perceiving

The judging (J) and perceiving (P) personality preferences focus on an individual's need for structure and closure.

Those who favor the judging function prefer to seek closure on issues sooner rather than later and to resolve things with "all deliberate speed." When dealing with family problems they want to get to the heart of the issues as soon as possible and then make decisions. Judging types can become irritated when important problems are put on hold or key decisions are postponed.

Judging types tend to maintain their possessions in an organized fashion. They will often hang up their clothes when rather than drop them in chairs. They tend to arrange their closet and drawers so it is easy to find what they need on a moment's notice. Judging types frequently comment that they want to get household chores done early on a Saturday morning so that they can enjoy the rest of the weekend.

Perceiving types may also enjoy having their residences neat and orderly, but they typically have less need than judging types to maintain such a condition on a regular basis. Perceiving types seldom have a strong need for closure. They prefer to delay decisions so they can incorporate any additional information that might come forward. Perceiving types want to be sure that they have not overlooked anything that may relate to their decisions. When family problems develop, perceiving types will want time to analyze things and will strive to make sure the family avoids jumping to premature conclusions.

Although judging types may prefer to complete their chores early on a Saturday morning, many perceiving types would have a difficult time understanding the need to complete chores within such a tight time frame. Judging types might identify with the slogan "Just do it," while perceiving types might identify with "I'll get to it."

The different approaches to structure by judging types and perceiving types might become evident if an announcement were made that a manufacturing plant would close in six months for a mandatory summer vacation. Within several weeks of such an announcement many of the judging types would probably have identified their vacation destinations, made travel and hotel reservations, and put together detailed vacation itineraries. In contrast, many of the perceiving types would probably wait until their vacation was several days away before beginning to make travel arrangements. If they developed detailed itineraries they might well change them if new possibilities were to develop.

Family members with different preferences on the judging-perceiving dichotomy frequently have misunderstandings over established times for family outings. Judging types typically expect family events to begin at their scheduled times. They can become irritated if they have to wait for family members who do not show up on time. In sharp contrast, perceiving types tend to view scheduled starting times as general guidelines rather than more rigid deadlines and often have difficulty comprehending why their judging type relatives become so upset over slight delays.

Differences between judging types and perceiving types can often lead to misperceptions that family members are behaving in certain ways consciously and purposely. Candid discussions can help families clear up such misperceptions and to come up with reasonable compromises. For example, families might establish a time frame for a family dinner (e.g. between 6:30 and 7:30) rather than an exact seating time.

Problems may develop between judging types and perceiving types over the timing of decisions. Those who favor judging often assume that perceiving types are ignoring the need to make decisions. In contrast perceiving types often feel pressured by judging types to reach what they believe are premature decisions. Family members can benefit by discussing which decisions really do need to be addressed right away and which decisions can be postponed.

In the United States judging types slightly outnumber perceiving types. Open dialogue can substantially enhance mutual understanding and acceptance on the JP dichotomy.

Personality Types

Combining the preferences on the four scales of the MBTI identifies a person's "personality type." The four scales of the MBTI lead to 16 different personality types. Try to keep in mind that while we have particular personality preferences and share certain similarities with other people who have the same personality preferences, each of us is unique. Although the MBTI is a convenient way to consider some aspects of behavior, we are not "controlled" by our personality preferences.

Many people new to the concepts of personality type secretly believe that there is one correct type and fifteen alternatives that could easily be improved upon with a little work. It just so happens that their own personality types are the correct ones and all the others are off a little. This tendency can result in everyone in your family trying to improve everyone else rather than learning to accept and cherish type differences. When used as intended, the MBTI can help us understand and accept our own type preferences *and* understand and appreciate those of family members.

A combination of MBTI preferences into a four letter designation (e.g., ISTJ) is the most common approach for considering a person's personality type. However, concentrating on one or two dimensions of personality preferences can also be useful. We will consider two such alternative approaches: dominant and inferior functions, and cognitive orientations.

Most and Least Preferred Functions

Jung suggested that each of us has a strong preference towards one of the four alternatives contained within the perceptual and decision-making dichotomies: sensing, intuition, thinking, or feeling. This function, which Jung called the dominant function, serves as a guiding light for our mental activities.

Jung suggested that each of us also has an inferior function which is always the opposite of the dominant function. Thus, if we have sensing as a dominant function, intuition will be the inferior function. In a similar fashion, if thinking is a dominant function, the inferior function will be feeling. Jung indicated that we devote the least amount of energy to the inferior function, preferring to avoid it altogether if we could.

While many people find it difficult to remember family members' preferences on all four of the MBTI scales, it is much easier to remember dominant functions. Phrasing a request in language consistent with a relative's dominant function should increase the probability that the message will be understood. For example, if a family member has sensing as a dominant function you can use sensing terms such as "the fact is..." or "the reality of the situation is...." In a similar fashion if a family member's dominant function is thinking, then you might say "the logical approach to this problem involves ...," or you might emphasize your desire to be "objective."

You may want to refrain from stressing things that are consistent with relatives' inferior functions. If a family member has feeling as an inferior function then you want to avoid focusing on the subjective impact a decision may have on loved ones. If a family member's inferior function is intuition, don't focus on future possibilities, because doing so will probably decrease the chance of being understood.

To help you identify the more preferred and less preferred functions, a quick reference guide is provided on the next page.

Cognitive Orientations

Focusing on dominant functions is much easier than trying to remember a family member's four MBTI preferences. Concentrating on dominant functions allows you to address either a perceptual preference (sensing or intuition) *or* a decision-making preference (thinking or feeling). If you want to enhance your communications a little more without remembering all four MBTI preferences, you can focus on both perceptual *and* decision-making preferences. A combination of perceptual and decision-making preferences is referred to as a person's cognitive orientation. There are four cognitive orientations:

Sensing & Thinking	ST
Sensing & Feeling	SF
Intuition & Thinking	NT
Intuition & Feeling	NF

Relatives who maintain a sensing and thinking (ST) cognitive orientation usually prefer to focus on existing realities and to make decisions logically and objectively. STs want to be sure all the facts are considered and that solutions are worked out systematically. For example, STs might concentrate on the details of a family member's recently diagnosed illness and the logical way to organize a pattern of family support during treatment. Should a natural disaster destroy a family residence, STs might focus on taking pictures of the damage and then developing a systematic way to obtain insurance reimbursement.

Those who favor the sensing and feeling (SF) cognitive orientation also tend to concentrate on immediate realities, but they usually want to address how immediate situations will affect family members.

MOST AND LEAST PREFERRED FUNCTIONS
QUICK REFERENCE GUIDE

PERSONALITY TYPE:	MOST FAVORED FUNCTION:		LEAST FAVORED FUNCTION:	
ISTJ	SENSING	(S)	INTUITION	(N)
ISFJ	SENSING	(S)	INTUITION	(N)
INFJ	INTUITION	(N)	SENSING	(S)
INTJ	INTUITION	(N)	SENSING	(S)
ISTP	THINKING	(T)	FEELING	(F)
INFP	FEELING	(F)	THINKING	(T)
ISFP	FEELING	(F)	THINKING	(T)
INTP	THINKING	(T)	FEELING	(F)
ESTP	SENSING	(S)	INTUITION	(N)
ESFP	SENSING	(S)	INTUITION	(N)
ENFP	INTUITION	(N)	SENSING	(S)
ENTP	INTUITION	(N)	SENSING	(S)
ESTJ	THINKING	(T)	FEELING	(F)
ENTJ	THINKING	(T)	FEELING	(F)
ESFJ	FEELING	(F)	THINKING	(T)
ENFJ	FEELING	(F)	THINKING	(T)

In the examples above, SFs might concentrate on how the ill relative was coping and how well other family members were reacting to the diagnosis. In the case of a natural disaster, an SF would probably concentrate on how relatives were coping with the emotional trauma of the moment.

Those who favor the intuitive and thinking (NT) cognitive orientation usually like to think about future possibilities and to work out their visions logically. With the family illness, NTs might direct discussions toward the probability for recovery and then develop a systematic plan for coping with the alternatives. In the case of the natural disaster, NTs might well develop a list of alternatives for securing long-term shelter rather than concentrating on immediate needs.

Those who favor an intuitive and feeling (NF) cognitive orientation usually prefer to concentrate on future possibilities that may affect relatives. NFs want to help create a positive future for loved ones. In the case of the ill relative, NFs would probably focus attention on the possibility of a full recovery while at the same time helping family members prepare for alternative outcomes. In the case of the natural disaster, NFs would probably concentrate first on helping family members visualize a bright new home and then help them cope with the emotional trauma being experienced.

If at all possible, it is best to focus on personality preferences across all four MBTI dimensions. If that is not practical, then identifying dominant functions is good, and working with cognitive orientations is even better (see chart below).

DIMENSION	EASE OF USE	EFFECTIVENESS
DOMINANT FUNCTION (S,N,T,F)	EASIEST	GOOD
COGNITIVE ORIENTATIONS (ST,SF,NT,NF)	MORE DIFFICULT	BETTER
PERSONALITY TYPE (FOUR LETTER COMBINATIONS E.G., ISTJ)	MOST DIFFICULT	BEST

Listening Across Type Differences

Up to this point we have concentrated on understanding personality preferences. Accepting our personality differences is important but, by itself, is inadequate to achieve genuine understanding. Active listening is also necessary to ensure that successful communications take place.

Learning to listen across type differences is a skill that few people master. A number of hurdles can stand in the way of your ability to understand what relatives are trying to communicate. Several suggestions for increasing your listening skills are provided below.

1. Give Your Full Attention to the Speaker.

When a relative is speaking we often pretend to listen while we are actually preparing our responses. Active listening, or concentrating all of our attention on speakers, is just plain hard work. You can improve your listening skills by blocking out external and internal distractions. For example, as soon as you catch yourself planning a response while someone else is talking, ask the speaker to repeat what was just said. Simply admit that "All of a sudden I got this idea and I'm afraid I might have missed something important." Another helpful thing to do when you catch your mind wandering is to focus on something the speaker is wearing. This will bring you back to the here-and-now and focus on the speaker.

2. Clarify What the Speaker Said: "Check it Out."

Once someone has finished speaking, ask for clarification of any statements that you are not sure you understood. This is called "checking it out" and is very important for effective listening. For example, if a family member claims to need something "right away" you might ask if "right away" means "by lunch," "by the end of the day," or "by the end of the week." If a relative suggests the two of you should have lunch together "soon" you might clarify whether that means "this week," "this month," or "before the end of the year." Ask politely, but be sure you leave with a clear understanding of what is expected.

3. Remember Type Differences in Communications.

Effective listening involves acceptance of, and accommodating for, personality differences in our communications. There are many ways in which type differences can affect us. For example, extraverts tend to "think out loud" when developing their opinions. In contrast, introverts often want time to reflect on issues before expressing their opinions. Since introverts give so much thought to issues before communicating with others, they tend to give greater weight to statements of extraverts than the extraverts may have intended. An introvert may say to an extravert, "A minute ago you took one position and now you have suddenly changed your mind in mid-stream." The extravert might respond, "You're right, but what's the problem?" Our many differences in personality preferences reinforce the need to "check it out."

4. Differentiate the Objective From The Emotional Content.

Some of the time our communications focus on objective aspects of issues, while at other times the subjective aspects take center stage. Try to interpret statements in their proper context. Don't anticipate that everything family members say is meant to be taken at face value. For example, a relative who is a passionate fan of a professional sports team might claim that the team's loss to a bitter rival was no big deal. As a more neutral observer of the team's chances of making the playoffs you might objectively agree with this assessment, only to miss the subtle devastation your relative is trying to conceal.

Another common mistake is to give candid or "honest" feedback when family members ask for your opinions. Sometimes we confuse our subjective evaluations with objective reality. For example, relatives may ask if you like new articles of clothing they have purchased. As beauty is in the eye of the beholder your opinions on their clothing are no more objective than anyone else's. Since they have already paid for the merchandise there is little to be gained by indicating you think the clothes look terrible. Often "Does this look good???" really means "Doesn't this look good!!!"

5. Take Responsibility For Your Interpretations.

Finally, you as the listener must take responsibility for your interpretations of family members' communications. Our interpretations are influenced by our academic training, personal history, personality preferences and many other factors. For example, if a relative suggests that balancing a check book on a regular basis is not important in the greater scheme of life, and you favor sensing, you might take offense at such an attitude. In a similar fashion, if a family member suggests that it is useless to anticipate what might develop in the future, and you favor intuition, you might disagree. In the end it is your perception of what was said by relatives that will guide your actions, not necessarily what they intended to communicate.

Communicating Across Type Differences

Acknowledging differences in personality types as an interference to effective communication is very important. A reference guide is provided on the following pages to help you enhance the effectiveness of your communications with those who may not share your personality type preferences.

REMINDERS FOR COMMUNICATING ACROSS TYPE DIFFERENCES:

Extraverted types tend to "think out loud" when forming opinions. Avoid making assumptions that initial statements by extraverts are their final position on an issue.

Ineffective phrasing "Read Mom's letter then tell me exactly what you think she means."

Effective phrasing "Read Mom's letter and then we can talk about what she might mean."

Introverted types are less comfortable than extraverts sharing issues of a personal nature. Give them time to collect their thoughts before asking them to respond.

Ineffective phrasing "I'll wait while you read Mom's letter and then we can discuss what it might mean."

Effective Phrasing "Why don't you read Mom's letter and then let me know when you are ready to discuss what she might mean."

Sensing types concentrate on facts and existing realities, so attempts to focus on the long-term ramifications of decisions are seldom effective. Phrase issues in the here-and-now language sensing types are comfortable with.

Ineffective phrasing "Just think of the possibilities if Mary were to get better grades."

Effective phrasing "We need to discuss actions we can take to encourage Mary to earn better grades."

Intuitive types want to focus on the future, so it isn't helpful to try to force intuitives to concentrate on the present. Reword questions or issues in terms that allow the intuitive listener to consider a variety of possibilities.

Ineffective phrasing "We really need to focus on solving this problem today."

Effective phrasing "Let's think of what might develop if we don't solve this problem today."

21 FAMILIES: USING TYPE TO ENHANCE MUTUAL UNDERSTANDING

Thinking types place a high value on the process by which conclusions are made. Let them explain their decision-making process to you, and ask if they have any questions about how you reached your decisions.

Ineffective phrasing	"The approach the family should take is obvious."
Effective phrasing	"Let me explain how I decided this is the right approach for the family to take."

Feeling types focus on the impact of decisions on the parties involved, not on whether the decisions will be consistent with past or future actions. Have them use their insights into people's reactions to decisions as a way to make logical choices.

Ineffective phrasing	"In order to be fair we should spend the same amount on each grandchild's birthday."
Effective phrasing	"How might our other grandchildren react if we spent a little extra for Johnny since he will be in the hospital on his birthday?"

Judging types have a strong need to wrap up decisions with all deliberate speed, so they can become irritated if issues are left open for long periods of time. Discuss which issues can be resolved in the immediate future and which issues you need more time to think about.

Ineffective phrasing	"Please don't ask me to make a decision before I'm ready."
Effective phrasing	"I understand that you want me to make a decision on which car we should buy and I will respond as soon as I can."

Perceiving types have little need to wrap up open issues so they prefer to postpone decisions to allow for new information that might be forthcoming. Differentiate between which issues are most important and which issues you can agree to postpone.

Ineffective phrasing	"We have to settle these issues today!"
Effective phrasing	"Let's look over all of the issues and agree on which ones we will settle now and which ones we can work on later."

Family Norms

Every family develops certain ways of interacting with each other that are unique to the family. They develop expected ways of carrying on daily life and have rituals for celebrating the holidays.

When people enter extended families, it often takes time for the newcomers to become familiar with family norms. For example, those who come from families of extraverts may have difficulty becoming comfortable with families that favor introversion. Extraverted families tend to carry on simultaneous conversations, but introverted families tend to have one person speak at a time while other family members listen. In a similar fashion, individuals who come from families that favor intuition may have difficulty adjusting to families that favor sensing. If intuitives share all the multiple versions of future possibilities they are likely to envision, sensing-oriented family members view them as losing touch with reality.

A couple can help each other adjust to their respective families by discussing family norms and psychological preferences. Discussing such differences can help speed along the adjustment process.

We will now review the sixteen individual type descriptions associated with the Myers-Briggs Type Indicator.

Understanding the Sixteen Types

ISTJ

Those who favor the ISTJ personality type tend to take a quiet approach to enjoying life's realities. Their introversion leads them to reflect on issues prior to sharing their opinions with others. A preference for sensing leads to a focus on the here-and-now and being certain of the circumstances. ISTJs typically work through issues systematically and then seek closure as soon as practical.

When working through family problems, ISTJs will often step back and reflect before making any statements. When they feel prepared, they will join family discussions and will seek to explore the circumstances that led to the conflicts. Although they are concerned with family members' feelings, their preference for thinking will lead ISTJs to present their opinions logically and objectively without regard for the emotional aspects of disputes.

The most favored function for ISTJs is sensing. As a result, they concentrate on the full range of facts and details connected with family issues. Their least favored function is intuition, so they usually have little desire to focus on future possibilities.

ISTJs want to be appreciated for their practical, dependable and consistent approach to family affairs. They often serve as a resource on family history and traditions and can recall the most distant family conversations on a moment's notice. ISTJs want their lives to run smoothly and to stick with proven ways of doing things. Their focus on traditions leads them to object to trying new approaches unless there are demonstrated needs to do so.

When communicating with ISTJs, begin by carefully restating the important facts. Provide details, include references to precedents whenever possible, and then indicate that you are willing to wait until they have had a chance to reflect on the issues.

When asking ISTJs to share opinions, keep in mind that ISTJs do not "shoot from the hip." They want to think about problems before offering responses.

ISTJs are generally not very demonstrative. They often fail to perceive a need to provide verbal reassurances of love or support to family members. Do not be surprised if ISTJ relatives assume that the warm welcome expressed during your marriage ceremony was adequate to ensure your feeling part of the family.

As your relationships with ISTJs develop over time, you will probably find it easier to recognize and appreciate the depth of their grasp of reality and analytical skills. Their remarkable grasp of the facts surrounding issues may help family members avoid overlooking critical points in difficult family crises. Over time ISTJs may become viewed as quiet, reliable and thoroughly dependable members of the family.

ISFJ

Those who favor the ISFJ personality type tend to take a quiet approach to enjoying their life as it develops. Their introversion leads them to reflect on issues before sharing their opinions. A preference for sensing results in their concentrating on the here-and-now and all that is going on around them. ISFJs typically focus on the ways decisions affect other people, and they tend to seek closure as soon as practical.

When working through family problems, ISFJs often step back and reflect before sharing their thoughts. When they feel prepared, they will join in family discussions and will seek to explore the circumstances that led to the problems. They will use their considerable interpersonal skills to find solutions acceptable to everyone involved in the conflicts.

ISFJs want to be appreciated for the deep and genuine support they freely offer to family members. They will usually go to great lengths to ensure that family events run smoothly, often personally taking on a disproportionate amount of the work. They will quietly provide support to any family members they perceive as being upset or just emotionally down.

The most favored function for ISFJs is sensing. As a result, ISFJs spend a great deal of effort concentrating on the facts involved with situations. They frequently provide the most intricate and detailed information and do so from memory. Their least favored function is intuition, so they usually devote little effort to contemplating future scenarios.

When communicating with ISFJs, begin by carefully restating the facts. Be certain to discuss your interpretations of how others are responding to conflicts and how you feel the issues can be resolved in a manner acceptable to all involved. Close by saying the ISFJs can have as long as they need to reflect on the problems.

Remember when asking for their opinions that ISFJs rarely "shoot from the hip." They want to think about the facts and ramifications of suggested actions before sharing their thoughts. Trying to speed up responses from ISFJs often leads to further hesitation on their part.

Many individuals find it difficult to understand the subtle and infrequent expressions of support by ISFJs. ISFJs often hold deep affections for family members, but find it difficult to express their emotions verbally. However, those who share a desire for expressions of support and inclusion find that ISFJs will make every effort to fulfill those needs.

As your relationships with ISFJs develop over time, you will probably find it easier to recognize the depth of their feelings. Their near total grasp of the facts surrounding issues may help family members avoid overlooking critical aspects of family problems. Over time ISFJs may become perceived as quiet, well informed, and very sensitive members of the family.

INFJ

Those who favor the INFJ personality type tend to take a quiet approach to enjoying life's possibilities. Their introversion leads them to reflect on issues before sharing opinions. A preference for intuition results in a focus on the future and all the various possibilities that may develop over time. INFJs typically concentrate on the impact decisions may have on others, and they seek closure as soon as possible.

When working through family problems, INFJs often step back and reflect before sharing their thoughts. When they feel prepared, they will join in family discussions by offering a variety of alternatives for resolving conflicts.

INFJs want to be appreciated for their innovative nature and their ability to come up with solutions acceptable to everyone involved in a dispute. They may care deeply for family members, but may not be known for frequently expressing their affections. They enjoy solving complex interpersonal issues and will quietly seek family consensus to resolve any lingering family disputes. INFJs may take family conflicts personally rather than being objective about their role in such situations.

The most favored function for INFJs is intuition. As a result, they place great value on developing innovative approaches to anything that interests them. Their least favored function is sensing, so they often overlook details. When INFJs say they didn't see something (such as a misspelled word), or they forget things (like relatives' birthdays), they are probably being sincere. Sensing types sometimes find it difficult to understand INFJs' difficulties with facts and figures.

When communicating with INFJs, begin by sharing various alternatives for solving problems. Focus on your interpretation of others' reactions to family conflicts and how you feel problems can be resolved in ways acceptable to everyone involved. Close by telling the INFJs you are ready to move on the problem when they are.

When asking for opinions, remember that INFJs often want to focus on alternative possibilities. They usually want to think about their responses before sharing them with others. Trying to hurry decisions from INFJs often slows down their decision making process.

It may be difficult to recognize and understand INFJs' ways for expressing love, support and inclusion towards other family members. Relatives' desires for expressions of support frequently go undetected by INFJs. However, once INFJs recognize such needs they will often provide feedback in a very sincere manner.

As your relationships with INFJs develop over time, you will probably find it easier to recognize the depth of their feelings. Their keen insights regarding alternative possibilities to problems may help the family avoid overlooking novel approaches to resolving conflicts. Their ability to anticipate the emotional reactions of others should help improve family harmony. Over time INFJs may become perceived as quiet, highly creative and very sensitive members of the family.

INTJ

Those who favor the INTJ personality type tend to take a quiet approach to enjoying life's possibilities. Their introversion leads them to reflect before sharing their opinions. A preference for intuition results in a desire to explore various possibilities, while their thinking preference encourages a systematic and logical analysis of the alternatives for solving problems. INTJs will frequently seek closure on issues as soon as possible.

When working through family problems, INTJs will usually reflect prior to sharing their thoughts. When they decide they are ready to participate, they will join in family discussions by exploring a variety of alternatives for resolving the issues at hand. Although they are concerned with the feelings of family members, their preference for thinking leads them to present their opinions logically and objectively rather than focusing on subjective factors.

INTJs want to be appreciated for their innovative nature and their ability to develop logical, well-structured and creative solutions. They frequently identify flaws and inconsistencies in complex family plans. INTJs often point out problems in family members' proposals without recognizing that they may be offending their relatives in the process.

The most favored function for INTJs is intuition. As a result, they place a strong emphasis on developing innovative solutions to problems. INTJs' visions are almost always logically structured. Their least favored function is sensing, so they often overlook details. When INTJs say they didn't see something (such as a misspelled word), or they forget things (like relatives' birthdays), they are probably being sincere. Sensing types sometimes find INTJs' problems with facts and figures difficult to understand.

When communicating with INTJs, focus on future implications associated with potential courses of action. Work through each possibility in a logical and systematic manner. Conclude by stating that INTJs can take as much time as they need to consider the issues.

When asking for opinions, keep in mind that INTJs do not "shoot from the hip." They usually want time to think about the ramifications of alternative courses of action before they provide their conclusions.

It may be difficult to recognize and understand INTJs' expressions of love and support for family members. INTJs may not perceive a need to provide verbal reassurances that relatives are valuable additions to the family. Do not be surprised if your INTJ relatives assume that the warm welcome expressed during your marriage ceremony was adequate to ensure your feeling as a full-fledged family member.

As your relationships with INTJs develop over time, you will probably find it easier to recognize the depth of their visions. Their keen insights regarding the implications surrounding issues may lead to creative approaches to solving family problems. Over time INTJs may become perceived as quiet, highly creative and very logical members of the family.

ISTP

Those who favor the ISTP personality type tend to take a quiet approach to enjoying life's realities. Their introversion leads them to reflect on issues before sharing their opinions. A preference for sensing results in a focus on the here-and-now and being certain of the facts surrounding issues. Their preference for thinking leads them to work through issues logically and objectively, while their preference for perceiving encourages them to stay with the issues until they have had ample time to review all the facts.

When working through family problems, ISTPs will usually reflect before they are willing to provide their thoughts. When they are prepared, they will join in family discussions, often by asking penetrating questions that explore the circumstances which led to the problems. Although ISTPs may be concerned with family members' feelings, their preference for thinking leads them to focus on presenting their ideas logically and objectively.

ISTPs want to be appreciated for their ability to systematically process the numerous facts and myriad details associated with family issues. They are typically able to simplify huge amounts of diverse data and present the relevant facts in ways that help family members better understand the complexities of difficult problems.

The most favored function for ISTPs is thinking. As a result, ISTPs tend to concentrate their energies on ensuring that problems are considered objectively. Their least favored function is feeling, so they might overlook the reactions their suggestions may create in others. When ISTPs say that they didn't realize how relatives would react to a suggestion, they are probably being sincere.

When communicating with ISTPs, begin by carefully restating the facts. Provide details, include references to precedents whenever possible, and then assure them they can have as much time as they would like to reflect on the issues.

When asking for opinions, keep in mind that ISTPs do not "shoot from the hip." They want time to reflect on issues before providing their reactions. Trying to force responses from ISTPs is often counterproductive.

It may be difficult to recognize and understand ISTPs' expressions of love and support for family members. ISTPs may have strong feelings towards other family members, but may find it very difficult to verbalize them.

As your relationships with ISTPs develop over time, you will probably find it easier to recognize the depth of their grasp of reality and their analytical skills. Their keen insights regarding the facts surrounding issues can help family members avoid missing critical aspects of difficult problems. Over time ISTPs may become perceived as quiet, logical and highly dependable members of the family.

ISFP

Those who favor the ISFP personality type tend to take a quiet approach to enjoying life's realities. Their introversion leads them to reflect on issues before sharing their opinions. A preference for sensing results in a focus on the here-and-now and being sure of the details associated with issues. ISFPs usually focus their attention on the impact problems are having on others, rather than concentrating on the objective facts involved. They will usually take as much time as they feel necessary to thoroughly review issues before coming to conclusions.

When working through family problems, ISFPs generally want to reflect before sharing their thoughts. When they feel they are prepared, they will join in family discussions by asking penetrating questions that explore the circumstances which led to problems being considered.

ISFPs want to be appreciated for their deep loyalty to family members and their concern for everyone's feelings. They tend to evaluate issues according to their strongly held personal values and will usually stick by those values, even at high costs to themselves. ISFPs often mask the depth of their feelings rather than share them verbally with family members.

The most favored function for ISFPs is feeling. As a result, they are extremely sensitive to the impact their decisions and actions may have on family members. Their least favored function is thinking, so they may experience difficulty talking out tough-minded analysis in a manner that is convincing to their relatives.

When communicating with ISFPs, begin by carefully restating the facts. Focus on your interpretation of how family members will respond to different courses of action and how you feel issues can be resolved in ways acceptable to everyone involved. Conclude by telling ISFPs that they can have as much time as they would like to reflect on the problems.

When asking for opinions, remember that ISFPs do not "shoot from the hip." ISFPs generally want time to reflect on issues before sharing their reactions. Trying to force decisions from ISFPs is usually counterproductive.

It may be difficult to recognize and understand ISFPs' expressions of love and support for family members. ISFPs may have strong feelings, but may find it extremely difficult to express those emotions verbally. This can sometimes be frustrating to family members, since they have learned over time that ISFPs are very sensitive.

As your relationships with ISFPs develop over time, you will probably find it easier to recognize the depth of their feelings. Their keen insights regarding the facts surrounding issues may help family members avoid overlooking critical aspects of difficult problems. Their ability to anticipate the emotional reactions of others will help smooth ruffled feathers within the family. Over time ISFPs may become perceived as quiet, insightful and very compassionate members of the family.

INFP

Those who favor the INFP personality type tend to take a quiet approach to enjoying life's possibilities. Their preference for introversion influences them to reflect on issues before sharing their opinions. Their preference for intuition leads them to explore a variety of possibilities that may or may not develop in the future. INFPs generally concentrate on the impact decisions may have on others and take as much time as necessary to review alternatives.

When working through family problems, INFPs usually want to reflect before sharing their thoughts. When they feel they are prepared, they will join in family discussions, often asking penetrating questions that explore possibilities for resolving issues. During the course of family disputes, INFPs may become very anxious to reach resolutions that leave everyone emotionally comfortable. It is sometimes hard to understand how difficult it is for INFPs to function in emotionally charged family situations.

INFPs want to be appreciated for their loyalty to family members and their ability to be quietly supportive of relatives in need. They will often go to great lengths to facilitate family harmony and will accept many personal sacrifices to achieve harmony. However, INFPs may react suddenly and even forcefully if their deeply held personal values are challenged. Even if INFPs develop a number of possibilities for resolving problems, they may refrain from attempting to persuade family members to adopt their suggestions.

The most favored function for INFPs is feeling. As a result, they can be extremely sensitive to the impact their decisions or actions may have on relatives. Their least favored function is thinking, so they may experience difficulty talking out tough-minded analysis in a manner that is convincing to their relatives.

When communicating with INFPs, begin by exploring the various alternatives to problems. Be certain to discuss your interpretation of how relatives are responding to problems and how you feel family members will react to the various alternatives you have identified. Close by informing INFPs that they can have as much time as they need to consider the options.

When asking for opinions, remember that INFPs do not "shoot from the hip." INFPs want time to reflect on issues before being asked to share their reactions.

It may be difficult to recognize and understand INFPs' expressions of love and support for family members. INFPs may hold strong feelings for relatives, but may find it difficult to express them verbally. INFPs will quietly try to demonstrate their love and support in ways that less sensitive family members may not notice.

As your relationships with INFPs develop you will probably find it easier to recognize the depth of their feelings. Their keen insights regarding the implications stemming from alternative courses of action may help family members avoid unintended outcomes. Their ability to anticipate the emotional reactions of others may enhance mutual understanding among family members. Over time INFPs may become perceived as quiet, insightful and highly sensitive members of the family.

INTP

Those who favor the INTP personality type tend to take a quiet approach to enjoying life's possibilities. Their introversion leads them to reflect on issues before sharing their opinions. Their preference for intuition results in a desire to explore a variety of future possibilities on any issues they consider. Their preference for thinking results in logical and systematic analyses of new possibilities. INTPs usually take time to ensure they have reviewed all the possibilities before reaching any conclusions.

When working through family problems, INTPs will often reflect before sharing their thoughts. When they decide that they are prepared to join family discussions, they may ask penetrating questions that explore a variety of alternatives for resolving issues. Although they may be concerned with family members' feelings, their preference for thinking leads them to present their options objectively.

INTPs want to be appreciated for their ability to develop fair and reasonable solutions to family problems. They often pull together other people's suggestions into coherent plans of action.

The most favored function for INTPs is thinking. As a result, they concentrate their energies on ensuring that issues are considered objectively. Their least favored function is feeling, so they may overlook the reactions their suggestions might have on others.

When communicating with INTPs, begin by reviewing several future implications associated with the issues being considered. Work through each implication in a logical and systematic manner. Conclude by indicating that they can have as much time as they would like before responding.

When asking for opinions, keep in mind that INTPs do not "shoot from the hip." For example, if you attend a play with an INTP in-law, and then ask for a reaction to the play, you may get only a casual comment or two at that point in time. Don't be surprised, however, if the INTP calls you at home two days later to engage in a thorough analysis of the play.

It may be difficult to recognize and understand INTPs' expressions of love, support and inclusion. INTPs may not perceive the need to provide verbal reassurances that relatives are valuable additions to the family. INTP relatives may assume that the warm welcome expressed during your marriage ceremony was adequate to ensure your feeling as a full-fledged family member. The need for expressions of inclusion frequently go undetected and unaddressed by INTPs.

As your relationships with INTPs develop over time you will probably find it easier to recognize and appreciate the depth of their feelings. Their keen insights regarding future possibilities surrounding issues may help family members think through the logical implications of suggested actions. Over time INTPs may become perceived as quiet, logical and insightful members of the family.

ESTP

Those who favor the ESTP personality type tend to share their enjoyment of life's realities in the presence of others. Their extraversion leads them to discuss topics with others before finalizing their own opinions. Their preference for sensing results in a focus on the here-and-now and on the facts related to issues. ESTPs prefer to think through matters logically and systematically and to discuss all aspects of issues before making up their minds.

When working through family problems, ESTPs usually encourage open discussions with everyone involved. They seek input from family members and will often encourage participation by relatives who are more reserved. ESTPs generally seek input from as many sources as possible before being willing to reach conclusions.

ESTPs like to focus on the facts associated with problems and will then process solutions systematically. Although they may be concerned with the feelings of family members, ESTPs typically approach problems logically and objectively.

ESTPs want to be appreciated for their ability to help organize family events. They may go to great lengths to have relatives included in important family matters. However, while they try to get everyone involved, they may be less sensitive to how family members are reacting to proposed solutions. ESTPs often get everyone participating, but bruise some feelings in the process.

The most favored function for ESTPs is sensing. As a result, they frequently have a tremendous grasp of the facts associated with family issues. The ability of ESTPs to recall a wealth of information often amazes those who do not share this personality type. The least favored function for ESTPs is intuition, so they often have difficulty anticipating the long-term ramifications of their actions.

When communicating with ESTPs, begin by carefully restating the facts. Provide details to support your positions and incorporate references to precedents whenever possible. Make sure you present things logically and objectively.

When seeking their opinions, keep in mind that ESTPs will want to discuss issues before they formulate reactions. Introverts sometimes have difficulty understanding why ESTPs want to discuss issues before having an opportunity to reflect on the facts. Sometimes ESTPs are accused of "shooting from the hip" or failing to reflect on important problems.

Except in moments of family crisis, ESTPs often do not recognize the need to express verbal reassurances of love, support and inclusion to family members. Relatives with such needs often find this difficult to understand, since they often perceive ESTPs as being very outgoing and spontaneous.

As your relationships with ESTPs develop over time it may become easier to recognize and appreciate the depth of their ability to handle details in a logical manner. Their keen insights regarding the facts surrounding issues may help family members identify solutions to difficult problems. Over time ESTPs are likely to be perceived as detail-oriented, logical and outgoing members of the family.

ESFP

Those who favor the ESFP personality type tend to share their enjoyment of life's realities in the presence of others. Their extraversion leads them to discuss topics with others before finalizing their opinions. A preference for sensing provides a focus on the here-and-now and the facts surrounding issues. ESFPs usually concentrate on the impact of decisions on everyone affected, and they generally take ample time to review all aspects of important issues before making up their minds.

When working through family problems, ESFPs often seek open-ended discussions with everyone involved. They want to join in careful consideration of how family members are affected by the problems and how they may be impacted by the alternative solutions. ESFPs typically assign only secondary importance to considering problems objectively. They will strive to make sure that the family does not jump to premature decisions on important issues.

ESFPs want to be appreciated for their ability to identify solutions to family issues that are acceptable to everyone in the family. The ability of ESFPs to accurately perceive what needs to be done to resolve conflicts often results in ingenious compromises. Their talents for smoothing over bruised feelings can help facilitate family harmony. ESFPs are often perceived as the family peacemakers. However, you must be careful not to assume that ESFPs will take the course of least resistance, or will join in decisions to resolve problems simply in order to avoid conflicts. When they are dealing with issues that are close to their hearts, ESFPs will usually stick to their beliefs and devote enormous effort to persuading others of the wisdom of their positions.

The most favored function for ESFPs is sensing. As a result, they frequently have a tremendous grasp of the facts associated with family issues. The ability of ESFPs to recall a wealth of information often amazes those who do not share this personality type. The least favored function for ESFPs is intuition, so they often have difficulty anticipating the long-term ramifications of their actions.

When communicating with ESFPs, begin by carefully restating the facts. Focus on the impact the proposed solutions may have on relatives, and then be willing to carry on extended discussions before seeking their opinions. In some cases ESFPs will provide their reactions during initial conversations, while in other cases they will want more time to consider the points brought up in your discussions.

As your relationships with ESFPs develop you will probably become more aware of the depth of their grasp of the details and their sensitive natures. ESFPs' keen insights into solving conflicts may contribute to family harmony. Over time ESFPs may become perceived as outgoing, detail-oriented and sensitive members of the family.

ENFP

Those who favor the ENFP personality type tend to share their love of life's possibilities in the presence of others. Their extraversion leads them to discuss topics before finalizing their opinions. A preference for intuition results in a strong desire to consider a variety of possibilities on things that interest them. ENFPs tend to concentrate on the impact of decisions on family members and will generally take ample time to review all aspects of proposed solutions before finalizing their opinions.

When working through family problems, ENFPs usually promote open discussions with everyone involved. They encourage others to join in a careful consideration of how family members may be affected by the alternative solutions being considered. ENFPs often assign only secondary importance to approaching problems objectively.

ENFPs want to be appreciated for their ability to create innovative solutions to practically any issues they encounter. Once they decide on courses of action they will typically go about generating enthusiasm for their initiatives among family members. ENFPs are usually willing to alter their courses of action as developing circumstances dictate. This sometimes leads relatives to perceive ENFPs as inconsistent or "fickle." Do not assume that ENFPs will go along with anything just to maintain harmony. If problems affect their deeply help beliefs, ENFPs will strive with all their energy to convince others of the correctness of their positions.

The most favored function for ENFPs is intuition. As a result, their lives revolve around the creation and/or identification of new possibilities. Family members who do not share the ENFP personality type often express concern that ENFP relatives seem to be out of touch with reality since they come up with so many new initiatives or "wild ideas." ENFPs do not expect all of their ideas to be realized. They focus on what *could* happen rather than what necessarily *will* happen in the future.

The least favored function for ENFPs is sensing, which frequently results in their overlooking critical details of important issues. When ENFPs indicate that they simply did not recognize important points, it is safe to assume that they are being sincere.

When communicating with ENFPs, begin by reviewing a number of possible solutions. Focus on the impact of the various options on family members and then be willing to carry on a long and subjectively oriented conversation.

When you ask for opinions, remember that ENFPs want to discuss issues before they finalize their thoughts. This facet of their behavior contrasts with the behavior of introverts, who are prone to reflect on issues before expressing their reactions. Sometimes ENFPs will express opinions during the course of conversations, while at other times they will want to think about points that came up during your discussions.

As your relationships with ENFPs develop you will probably find that you no longer become upset when they change their minds during the course of conversations. Their desire to project numerous possibilities should no longer cause you to question their grasp on reality. Their keen insights regarding the implications associated with various alternatives may help the family reach satisfactory solutions to problems. Over time ENFPs may become perceived as outgoing, visionary and sensitive members of the family.

ENTP

Those who favor the ENTP personality type tend to share their enjoyment of life's possibilities in the presence of others. Their extraversion leads them to discuss topics before finalizing their opinions. Their preference for intuition results in a focus on future possibilities. ENTPs usually prefer to think through matters logically and systematically, and they will generally take ample time to review all aspects of issues before making up their minds.

When working through family problems, ENTPs will typically promote open discussions with everyone involved. Their preference for thinking leads them to concentrate on the objective aspects of problems and to assign less importance to the impact of those decisions. ENTPs will often seek to focus family discussions on the future impacts of various alternatives, with little interest in the historical details related to issues.

ENTPs want to be appreciated for their ability to generate systematic and objective approaches to solving family problems. Once they have identified solutions they will usually work non-stop to implement their plans. Although energetic and determined,

ENTPs may become so focused that they offend relatives they are trying to assist. They will use their considerable energy to get problems resolved, but may bruise some feelings in the process.

The most favored function for ENTPs is intuition. As a result, their lives revolve around the creation and/or identification of new possibilities. They love to work out logical ways to implement their many visions of the future. The least favored function for ENTPs is sensing, which leads to their overlooking, or simply missing, details associated with their many endeavors. When ENTPs indicate that they missed important points, they are probably being sincere.

When communicating with ENTPs, begin by reviewing several logically thought-out solutions to the issues being considered. Demonstrate the logic of your solutions, avoid depending on references to precedents, and then be willing to carry on a long discussion. Do not take it personally when ENTPs abruptly point out flaws in the organization of your ideas, since such insights seem to burst out of ENTPs rather than having been calculated to offend.

When you ask their opinions, remember that ENTPs will usually want to discuss issues before finalizing their positions. On some occasions ENTPs will tell you their reactions during initial discussions, while at other times they will want to consider the points brought up during your conversations.

Even though ENTPs freely share their analyses of situations, they are much less likely to provide verbal assurances of love and support to family members. Except in moments of family crisis, ENTPs often do not recognize the desires of relatives for verbal reassurances.

As your relationships with ENTPs develop it will probably become easier to recognize and appreciate the depth of their creative and analytical talents. Their keen insights regarding the possibilities surrounding issues may help the family develop innovative approaches to resolving problems. Over time ENTPS may become perceived as outgoing, insightful and creative members of the family.

ESTJ

Those who favor the ESTJ personality type tend to share their enjoyment of life's realities in the presence of others. Their extraversion leads them to discuss topics with others before finalizing their opinions. A preference for sensing results in a focus on the here-and-now and a desire to obtain all of the facts related to issues. ESTJs typically prefer to think through matters systematically and to reach conclusions as soon as practical.

When working through family problems, ESTJs will often promote open discussions with everyone involved. Although they may be concerned with the impact of decisions on family members, a preference for thinking leads ESTJs to concentrate on problems logically and objectively. ESTJs often attempt to focus family discussions on facts rather than on hypothetical possibilities.

ESTJs want to be appreciated for their ability to effectively manage the myriad of details involved with family activities. They will typically adopt an active approach to getting things done. The ability to organize various facets of family events will help make sure that everything runs on time. However, ESTJs have a tendency to express their displeasures if other family members are running behind schedule or seem to be disorganized. The tendency of ESTJs to be candid with their criticisms may add fuel to disputes rather than lead to their resolutions.

The most favored function for ESTJs is thinking. As a result, ESTJs usually concentrate their energies on ensuring that family problems are considered logically. They want to be sure that everyone is treated fairly and consistently. The least favored function for ESTJs is feeling, so they may overlook the implications their suggestions may have for relatives. Be careful not to assume that perceived slights by ESTJs are intentional. ESTJs can become so absorbed in tasks that they are simply unaware of how they are affecting family members.

When communicating with ESTJs, begin by carefully restating the facts. Provide details to support your positions, incorporate references to precedents whenever possible, and then be willing to carry on a long discussion.

When you ask for opinions remember that ESTJs will probably want to discuss issues before finalizing their positions. On some occasions ESTJs will provide their reactions during initial discussions, while at other times they will want to consider points brought up during your conversations.

Even though ESTJs freely share their analyses of situations, they are much less likely to provide verbal assurances of their love or support for family members. Except in moments of family crisis, ESTJs seldom recognize family members' needs for verbal reassurances.

As your relationships with ESTJs develop, it will probably become easier to recognize and appreciate the depth of their grasp of the facts and their ability to be objective during emotion-laden conflicts. Their near total grasp of the facts surrounding issues will help family members avoid overlooking critical aspects of difficult problems. Over time ESTJs may become perceived as outgoing, logical and dependable members of the family.

ESFJ

Those who favor the ESFJ personality type tend to share their enjoyment of life's realities in the presence of others. Their extraversion leads them to discuss topics before finalizing their opinions. A preference for sensing provides a focus on the here-and-now and the factual circumstances surrounding issues. ESFJs concentrate on the impact of decisions on everyone involved and will usually seek closure as soon as practical.

When working through family problems, ESFJs typically promote open discussions with everyone involved. They encourage relatives to join in careful considerations of how family members are affected by the original problems and recommended solutions. ESFJs tend to focus on the impact of solutions on family members and to assign only secondary importance to considering problems objectively. Although they strive to implement solutions that accommodate everyone, don't take it for granted that ESFJs will always accept the course of least resistance in order to avoid conflicts. ESFJs will usually stick with their opinions on matters they consider important and may devote a great deal of effort to persuading others to accept their positions.

The most favored function for ESFJs is feeling. As a result, ESFJs often have a knack to accurately perceive what needs to be done to help solve family conflicts. They frequently suggest ingenious compromises that permit family members to resolve heated disputes. The ability of ESFJs to smooth over bruised feelings often helps maintain family harmony. The least favored function for ESFJs is thinking, so they may have difficulty expressing their thoughts in ways that are easy for others to follow.

When communicating with ESFJs, begin by carefully restating the facts. Focus on the impact suggested solutions may have on family members and then indicate that you are willing to reach a decision as soon as they are ready.

When asking for opinions, remember that ESFJs usually like to discuss issues before they finalize their positions. On some occasions ESFJs will share their reactions during initial discussions, while at other times they will want to consider points brought up during your conversations.

As your relationships with ESFJs develop, you will probably recognize and appreciate the depth of their grasp on reality and their very sensitive natures. You may become less confused when ESFJs change their minds during conversations. The ability of ESFJs to identify compromises for difficult issues can help maintain family harmony. Over time ESFJs may become viewed as outgoing, factual and sensitive members of the family.

ENFJ

Those who favor the ENFJ personality type tend to share their enjoyment of life's possibilities in the presence of others. Their extraversion leads them to discuss topics before finalizing their opinions. A preference for intuition provides a focus on various possibilities. ENFJs typically concentrate on the impact of decisions on relatives, and they often seek closure as soon as possible.

When working through family problems, ENFJs often promote open discussions. They encourage everyone to join in careful considerations of how family members may be affected by the potential solutions. ENFJS typically focus on the impact of solutions and may assign only secondary importance to being objective. When they are confronting issues that are very important to them, ENFJs will usually stick to their positions rather than compromise, and will devote a great deal of effort to persuading others of the wisdom of their positions.

ENFJs generally believe they have the ability to accomplish almost anything they undertake. Often demonstrating incredible creativity in approaching tasks, they may devote unceasing energy to the pursuit of their dreams. Associating with ENFJs is exciting if you can keep up with the never ending series of new projects.

The most favored function for ENFJs is feeling. As a result, they frequently come up with numerous solutions to family problems. Most, if not all, of ENFJs' proposals are likely to be acceptable to the relatives involved with problems. Their least favored function is thinking, so they may have difficulty presenting their ideas in a manner that is easy for family members to follow.

When communicating with ENFJs, begin by reviewing a number of possible solutions. Focus on the impact the alternatives may have on family members and then indicate that you are willing to wrap things up as soon as they are ready.

When asking for opinions, remember that ENFJs will probably want to discuss issues before they finalize their positions. On some occasions ENFJs will share their reactions during initial discussions, while on other occasions they will want to consider points you brought up during your conversations.

When interacting with ENFJs remember that they like to consider what *could* happen in the future, not necessarily what *will* happen. Sometimes relatives consider ENFJs to be out of touch with reality since they tend to come up with so many new projects at one time.

As your relationships with ENFJs develop, you may become more accustomed to their many projects. Indeed, their need to project numerous possibilities should no longer cause you to doubt their grasp of reality. The ability of ENFJs to identify alternative solutions to difficult family problems should help contribute to family harmony. Over time ENFJs may become perceived as outgoing, sensitive and visionary members of the family.

ENTJ

Those who favor the ENTJ personality type tend to share their enjoyment of life's possibilities in the presence of others. Their extraversion leads them to discuss topics before finalizing their opinions. A preference for intuition provides a focus on various possibilities that might be pursued on any problems they consider. ENTJs typically concentrate on finding logical and systematic solutions to issues, and they will often seek closure as soon as possible.

When working through family problems, ENTJs often promote open discussions with everyone involved. They encourage relatives to join in a careful consideration of how problems can be resolved fairly and objectively. As a result of their desire to address issues objectively, their concern for the impact decisions may have on relatives frequently goes unstated.

ENTJs want to be appreciated for their ability to develop logical solutions to family problems. ENTJs generally believe they have the ability to accomplish almost anything they undertake, so long as they can use their reasoning powers to develop systematic solutions. Often demonstrating a great deal of creativity in approaching tasks, they devote unceasing energy to the pursuit of their dreams.

The most favored function for ENTJs is thinking. As a result, ENTJs usually concentrate their energies on ensuring that family problems are considered logically. They want to be sure that everyone is treated fairly and consistently. The least favored function for ENTJs is feeling, so they may overlook the implications their suggestions may have for relatives. Be careful not to assume that perceived slights by ENTJs are intentional. ENTJs can become so absorbed in tasks that they are simply unaware of how they are affecting family members.

When communicating with ENTJs, begin by reviewing a number of possible solutions. Focus on the logical organization of the proposed solutions, stress your desire to be fair and objective, and then be prepared to discuss the matter at length.

When asking for opinions, remember that ENTJs usually want to discuss issues before they finalize their positions. On some occasions ENTJs will tell you their reactions during your discussions, while on other occasions they will want to consider points you brought up during your conversations.

As your relationships with ENTJs develop, you will probably become more tolerant of their numerous initiatives and their occasional misreading of the impact of their actions on others. The ability of ENTJs to generate alternative approaches may help family members find better solutions to problems. Over time ENTJs may become perceived as outgoing, creative and logical members of the family.

Conclusion

Maintaining a harmonious family requires the good will and efforts of everyone in the family. The MBTI can help turn good intentions into effective communications through a mutual understanding of personality preferences.

As with all other endeavors in life that are worth pursuing, a solid grasp of the dynamics of communicating across type differences demands hard work. May the principles and insights you have gained from looking at type and family relationships help you build a brighter and more understanding future for each and every member of your family.

Appendix

Further Resources

There are a number of good resources for further information on psychological type and the application of psychological type to family relationships.

Gifts Differing by Isabel Briggs Myers with Peter B. Myers. Palo Alto, CA: Consulting Psychologists Press, 1990.

LifeTypes by Sandra Hirsh and Jean Kummerow. New York: Warner Books, 1989.

Navigating Midlife: Using Typology as a Guide by Eleanor S. Corlett and Nancy B. Millner. Palo Alto, CA: Consulting Psychologists Press, 1993.

One of a Kind: Making the Most of Your Child's Uniqueness by LaVonne Neff. Gainesville, FL: Center for Applications of Psychological Type, 1995.

People Types and Tiger Stripes (3rd edition) by Gordon Lawrence. Gainesville, FL: Center for Applications of Psychological Type, 1993.

The Developing Child by Elizabeth Murphy, Palo Alto, CA: Consulting Psychologists Press, 1992.

Type Talk by Otto Kroeger with Janet M. Thuesen. New York: Delacorte Press, 1988.

For further information on the
Myers-Briggs Type Indicator or to
purchase these books,
you may contact:

Center for Applications of Psychological Type
2815 N.W. 13th Street, Suite 401
Gainesville, FL 32609-2815
(904) 375-0160

Background Notes

The Author

Charles W. Ginn received his Ph.D. in Social Psychology from the University of Cincinnati in 1993 and serves as President of Cincinnati Venture Consultants. In addition to numerous academic and popular press articles on psychological type, Dr. Ginn has written two additional books on psychological type. *Voices of Loss*, developed in collaboration with the Beginning Experience International Lay Ministry, focuses on the impact of personality type preferences on the grieving process that accompanies the loss of a spouse through death or divorce.

Jung, Personality Type, and the Myers-Briggs Type Indicator is an introductory text on psychological type that has been adopted by the Central and Eastern European Center for Applied Psychology (CEECAP) for distribution within member countries. CEECAP, co-founded by Dr. Ginn and Dr. Cvetko Smilevski of Skopje, Macedonia, is collaborating with CAPT, Consulting Psychologists Press, and leading psychologists from member countries in the simultaneous interpretation and application of the MBTI through out Eastern Europe.

Dr. Ginn conducts numerous seminars on psychological type and enhancing family relationships, coping with the grieving process, and promoting teamwork within organizational settings. His family consists of his wife Janet and sons Patrick and Brendan.

Archdiocese of Cincinnati Family Life Office

Peg Black and Bonnie Mack of the Archdiocese of Cincinnati Family Life Office played a vital role in the development of *Families: Using Type to Enhance Mutual Understanding* and the *CAPT Family Relations Program*.

The Family Life Office conducts numerous marriage preparation and marriage enrichment programs. These efforts are coordinated with organizations within the Catholic community and many other denominations.

Peg Black has over fifteen years of experience in addressing various family issues at the parish, diocesean, and national levels. Peg and her husband Jack have two sons, Craig and Jeff.

Bonnie Mack has been involved in marriage preparation/enrichment, and ecumenical ministry for the past twelve years. She and her husband Tom have three children, Chris, Carrie, and Tim.

For further information on applications of the *CAPT Family Relations Program* in marriage preparation and marriage enrichment efforts, please contact the Archdiocese of Cincinnati Family Life Office, 100 East Eighth Street, Cincinnati, Ohio 45202, (513) 421-3131.

Center for Applications of Psychological Type, Inc. (CAPT)

The Center for Applications of Psychological Type, Inc. (CAPT) is a non-profit organization focused on the use of the Myers-Briggs Type Indicator and on the applications of psychological type. CAPT educates the public to view difference constructively by maintaining a number of services for use in education, counseling, organizational development, religious life, and research. CAPT computer scoring for the MBTI produces high-quality, professional reports. This service attracts a large number of MBTI users; it also facilitates the collection of MBTI responses, contribution significantly to original research on the study of personality.

If you would like to share a story or comments on applications of type in family settings for possible inclusion in future efforts, please forward them to the author in care of the Center for Applications of Psychological Type, Inc., 2815 NW 13th Street, Suite 401, Gainesville, Florida 32609, (904) 375-0160, FAX (904) 378-0503. We will need your name, MBTI profile, address, and telephone number.

MOST AND LEAST PREFERRED FUNCTIONS
QUICK REFERENCE GUIDE

PERSONALITY TYPE:	MOST FAVORED FUNCTION:		LEAST FAVORED FUNCTION:	
ISTJ	SENSING	(S)	INTUITION	(N)
ISFJ	SENSING	(S)	INTUITION	(N)
INFJ	INTUITION	(N)	SENSING	(S)
INTJ	INTUITION	(N)	SENSING	(S)
ISTP	THINKING	(T)	FEELING	(F)
INFP	FEELING	(F)	THINKING	(T)
ISFP	FEELING	(F)	THINKING	(T)
INTP	THINKING	(T)	FEELING	(F)
ESTP	SENSING	(S)	INTUITION	(N)
ESFP	SENSING	(S)	INTUITION	(N)
ENFP	INTUITION	(N)	SENSING	(S)
ENTP	INTUITION	(N)	SENSING	(S)
ESTJ	THINKING	(T)	FEELING	(F)
ENTJ	THINKING	(T)	FEELING	(F)
ESFJ	FEELING	(F)	THINKING	(T)
ENFJ	FEELING	(F)	THINKING	(T)